D1710337

A BASIC BOOK OF
GOLDFISH
LOOK-AND-LEARN

by
MARY SWEENEY

PHOTOGRAPHERS: Dr. Herbert R. Axelrod, Michael Gilroy,
B. Kahl, F. Rosenzweig, A. Roth

Distributed in the UNITED STATES to the Pet Trade by T.F.H. Publications, Inc., One T.F.H.
Plaza, Neptune City, NJ 07753; distributed in the UNITED STATES to the Bookstore and
Library Trade by National Book Network, Inc. 4720 Boston Way, Lanham MD 20706; in
CANADA to the Pet Trade by H & L Pet Supplies Inc., 27 Kingston Crescent, Kitchener,
Ontario N2B 2T6; Rolf C. Hagen Ltd., 3225 Sartelon Street, Montreal 382 Quebec; in
CANADA to the Book Trade by Macmillan of Canada (A Division of Canada Publishing
Corporation), 164 Commander Boulevard, Agincourt, Ontario M1S 3C7; in the United
Kingdom by T.F.H. Publications, PO Box 15, Waterlooville PO7 6BQ; in AUSTRALIA AND
THE SOUTH PACIFIC by T.F.H. (Australia), Pty. Ltd., Box 149, Brookvale 2100 N.S.W.,
Australia; in NEW ZEALAND by Brooklands Aquarium Ltd. 5 McGiven Drive, New
Plymouth, RD1 New Zealand; in Japan by T.F.H. Publications, Japan—Jiro Tsuda, 10-12-
3 Ohjidai, Sakura, Chiba 285, Japan; in SOUTH AFRICA by Multipet Pty. Ltd., P.O. Box
35347, Northway, 4065, South Africa. Published by T.F.H. Publications, Inc.
Manufactured in the United States of America by T.F.H. Publications, Inc.

OTHER BOOKS BY T.F.H.

TU-001, 64 pages
50 color photos

TW-107,
256 pages

SK-012, 64 pages
Over 65 color photos

YF-108, 32 pages

PS-874, 224 pages

SK-035, 64 pages

PS-663, 718 pages

PS-642, 446 pages

TS-177, 320 pages
350 color photos

TS-126, 430 pages, 1100+ photos

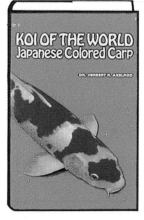
H-947, 239 pages, 327 color photos

PS-875, 144 pages 250 photos

H-1097, 800 pages
Over 1700 color photos

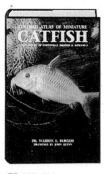
TS-183, 224 pages
356 color photos

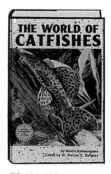
TS-161, 192 pages
640 color photos

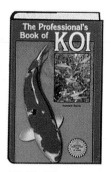
TS-158, 180 pages
Over 100 color photos

OTHER BOOKS BY T.F.H.

These and thousands of other animal books have been published by T.F.H. T.F.H. is the world's largest publisher of animal books. You can find our titles at the same place you bought this one, or write to us for a free catalog.

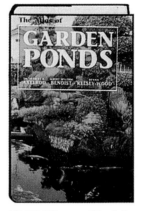

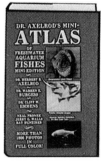

TU-016, 64 pages

H-1077, over 1150 pages
Over 7000 color photos

TS-178, 272 pages, 300+ photos

H-1090, 992 pages

TS-156, 128 pages
96 color photos

CO-017S, 128 pages

PB-112, 80 pages
29 color photos

TU-019, 64 pages

J-008, 48 pages
49 color photos

PL-2011, 360 pages
Over 400 color photos

PR-008, 32 pages

F-53, 32 pages
43 color photos

KW-048, 96 pages
58 color photos

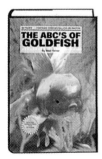

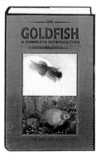

KW-153, 96 pages
58 color photos

T-104, 64 pages
64 color photos

CO-019S, 128 pages
136 color photos

CO-040S, 128 pages
191 color photos

H-909, 208 pages
125 color photos

INTRODUCTION

According to ancient Chinese records, the first goldfish was discovered about 300 A.D. The cultivation of the goldfish goes back about 1000 years when golden sports of crucian carp were first domesticated and bred in quantity for the pleasure of the nobility, who kept them in courtyard ponds. Soon, the offspring of the golden fish began to display tremendous variation in color and pattern. Through careful selection and hybridization, new varieties—with twin tails, long fins, or protruding eyes—were created from the simple carp. A new hobby was formed: goldfish keeping. Indeed, the Chinese have long loved the goldfish and included it in art and celebration.

◆ A portion of an 18th century Chinese mural painted on silk. Goldfish are often featured in Oriental art.

◆ The Japanese and Chinese kept goldfish in tubs where they could be viewed from above. This explains the emphasis on the appearance from the top rather than from the sides.

◆ A red crucian carp, also known as a hibuna. The crucian carp is the ancestor of many varieties of goldfish we know today.

◆ A Chinese teapot adorned with stylized goldfish.

INTRODUCTION

The goldfish hobby moved into Japan in about 1500, where goldfish were an instant hit and the Japanese goldfish hobby has a long and exciting history. Goldfish were on the move west, and the British, who thanks to Roman visitors had plenty of man-made ponds lying around, discovered goldfish to be wonderfully decorative in these ponds. It wasn't until the 1870s that goldfish immigrated to America, and by 1889 a goldfish farm had been established in Maryland. Again, the goldfish enjoyed a fabulous welcome. Now the goldfish is admired and kept worldwide and enjoys a solid position in the aquarium hobby.

➤ The Japanese are very taken with goldfish and they are often found in Japanese art.

◀ The beauty of fancy goldfish is celebrated in this beautiful silk print depicting an oranda and a telescope-eyed oranda.

The beautiful water lily is a perfect complement to fancy goldfish. ▶

INTRODUCTION

Goldfish are hardy, undemanding fish—for the most part. The common goldfish is as tough a fish as you are likely to get, but the more highly bred fancy varieties can be downright delicate.

These shiny pets have been kept in a wide assortment of containers, even chamber pots, but today most people keep their goldfish in aquaria or ponds. Fortunately, the days when people used to keep goldfish in the small glass "goldfish" bowls are gone. Even aquarium newcomers now know that it is impossible to maintain any kind of healthy water quality without a decent amount of water to work with.

The common goldfish in red and white makes a beautiful pet. It's very hardy and easy to care for.

◀ The Victorian era was famous for this sort of highly ornate household decoration. The use of a fountain and plants perhaps indicates that the fish were well cared for and lived long lives.

Round glass globes are not good for keeping fish of any sort. The water quality is very unstable and the small surface area cannot supply the amount of oxygen needed by even a single fish. ▶

To what lengths early aquarists were willing to go to keep their fishes happy! The "air pump" was a breakthrough in aquarium technology. ▶

Many of the goldfish varieties are winter-hardy and can spend their entire lives outdoors in ponds and pools provided the water doesn't freeze solid. This lovely pool is artistically arranged with bog plants and water lilies and stocked with goldfish. ▶

◀ This tiny pool is ideal for a few exquisite goldfish specimens. View-from-above varieties like celestials are ideal for a small, protected pool.

Bristol shubunkins are ideal pond fish. They are colorful, fast, and always hungry. A pond stocked with goldfish will never have a mosquito problem. ▶

INTRODUCTION

If your idea of a goldfish is the kind you used to get at county fairs or the 5&10, prepare your eyes. The goldfish varieties you will see on the following pages are beyond your wildest imagination.

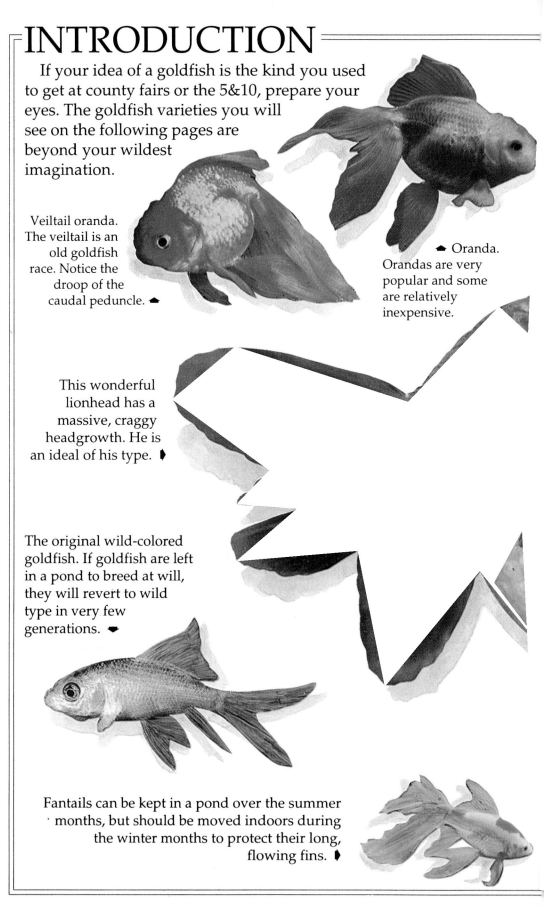

Veiltail oranda. The veiltail is an old goldfish race. Notice the droop of the caudal peduncle. ◄

◄ Oranda. Orandas are very popular and some are relatively inexpensive.

This wonderful lionhead has a massive, craggy headgrowth. He is an ideal of his type. ▶

The original wild-colored goldfish. If goldfish are left in a pond to breed at will, they will revert to wild type in very few generations. ◄

Fantails can be kept in a pond over the summer months, but should be moved indoors during the winter months to protect their long, flowing fins. ▶

◆ For most people, fantails are the first step into fancy goldfish.

◆ The common goldfish asks little of its keeper and will amply repay good care—that means a varied diet and regular partial water changes.

The more exotic the variety, the more carefully you must tend the fish. The celestial, for example, must have ideal conditions to thrive. ◆

The comet goldfish has introduced countless children and adults to the wider interests of the fishkeeping hobby. ◆

THE COLORS OF GOLD

Goldfish display their beauty through color, scales, and the shape of the eye, head, body, and fins. Beautiful and fascinating arrangements of color—red, white, gold, brown, black, blue, light yellow—dress the unusual and sometimes bizarre body of the goldfish.

◄ The fabulous red and white ryukin displays deep red coloration and iridescent, pure white scales. This is a great fish.

▶ Pearlscale goldfish have even rows of raised scales that have hard areas in the center of each scale. This is a very round-bodied fish. The double tail fin is square-cut like a veiltail, but much shorter.

The yellow-gold color of this lionhead is even and pure. Each scale is perfect. ◄

◄ The color of the headgrowth on the lionhead, or ranchu, is very important to breeders. The deeper the color, the more desirable.

The jikin, or peacock tail is a very old Japanese race of goldfish. The color on the fins should be solid red and the body solid white. This is one of the goldfish varieties that is as pleasing to view from above in a pond as it is from the side in an aquarium.

THE COLORS OF GOLD

How are these colors formed? Under a microscope, you would see that the colors on the goldfish's scales are composed of three substances: melanin, orange-red pigment, and light blue reflective substances called guanine.

◀ Blue pearlscale.

Rare black and red telescope-eye oranda fringetail. ➡

◀ A one-year-old veiltail with pleasing gold and white coloration.

▲ A magnificent pearlscale goldfish with square tail fins.

▲ Wild–type goldfish.

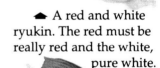

▲ A red and white ryukin. The red must be really red and the white, pure white.

◀ Ryukins.

A splendid black oranda.

◀ Chocolate oranda with nice headgrowth. Vegetable-based foods help keep good color in chocolate– or bronze–colored goldfish.

This very beautiful and rare variety is the Chinese fish named after the city in which it originated, Nanking. The butterfly tail and dorsalless back of this interesting breed make it a valuable addition to a pond. ➡

THE COLORS OF GOLD

These three substances in different combinations produce the colors of the goldfish's body. When melanin is entirely absent, orange-red pigment and guanine make a rich red color. When the melanin is abundant, you will have a black goldfish but you might see some of the orange-red pigment and guanine in gaps where the melanin is absent.

A trio of richly colored calico fantails with very nice finnage. ▶

◀ Rare blue–scaled butterfly with telescope eyes. The silvery scales are called blue.

▲ Rare albino telescope. The red iris indicates albinism.

Rare ermine (black and white) oranda. ▶

◀ Pearlscale going through color changes. The black and gray areas will soon be pure white.

This fish shows an interesting color pattern in an otherwise plain brown oranda. One year later, the entire fish turned to 100 percent deep orange-red. ▶

▲ Blue–scale oranda losing color. Blue turns to light gray or white.

◀ A diverse trio: pearlscale, oranda, and bubble-eye.

THE COLORS OF GOLD

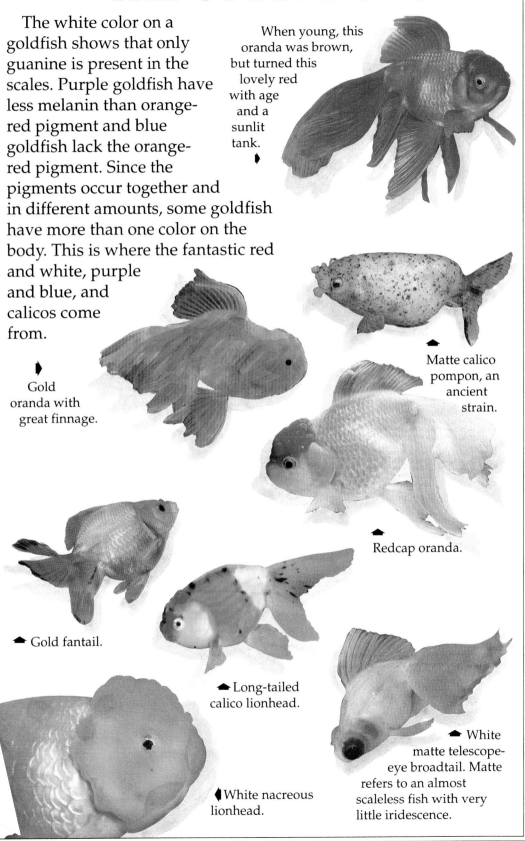

The white color on a goldfish shows that only guanine is present in the scales. Purple goldfish have less melanin than orange-red pigment and blue goldfish lack the orange-red pigment. Since the pigments occur together and in different amounts, some goldfish have more than one color on the body. This is where the fantastic red and white, purple and blue, and calicos come from.

When young, this oranda was brown, but turned this lovely red with age and a sunlit tank.

Gold oranda with great finnage.

Matte calico pompon, an ancient strain.

Redcap oranda.

Gold fantail.

Long-tailed calico lionhead.

White nacreous lionhead.

White matte telescope-eye broadtail. Matte refers to an almost scaleless fish with very little iridescence.

THE COLORS OF GOLD

The scales on a goldfish are "imbricated," which means they overlap like the roofing tiles on a house. The scales, which start at the head and go back to the region at the base of the tail (known as the caudal peduncle) provide protection for the fish.

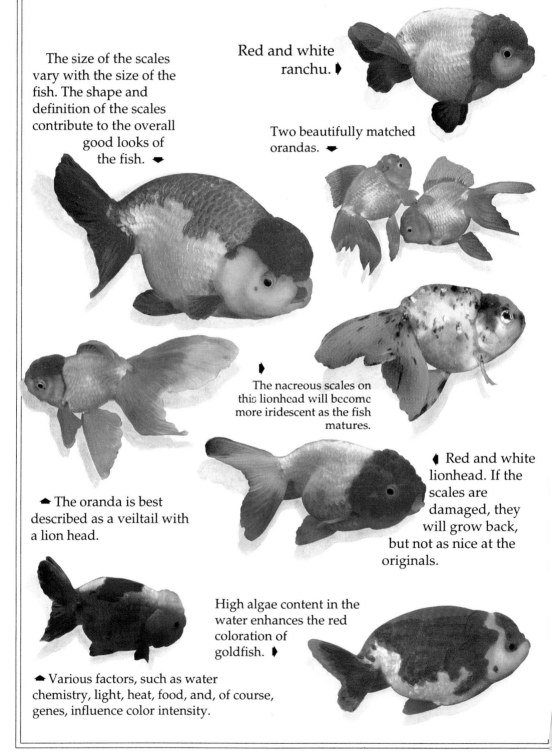

The size of the scales vary with the size of the fish. The shape and definition of the scales contribute to the overall good looks of the fish. ▶

Red and white ranchu. ▶

Two beautifully matched orandas. ▶

▶ The nacreous scales on this lionhead will become more iridescent as the fish matures.

◀ The oranda is best described as a veiltail with a lion head.

◀ Red and white lionhead. If the scales are damaged, they will grow back, but not as nice at the originals.

High algae content in the water enhances the red coloration of goldfish. ▶

▲ Various factors, such as water chemistry, light, heat, food, and, of course, genes, influence color intensity.

THE COLORS OF GOLD

The entire body of the goldfish is covered with a thin, protective slime. This slime is clear and shiny and is the first line of defense against disease. Stress and handling can remove parts of the slime coat. A good remedy for loss of slime coat is to put one teaspoon of salt for every two gallons of water until the fish is recovered. Then remove the salt through water changes.

An orange and white oranda with a spectacular tail and strong dorsal.

An orange and white oranda with white headgrowth and a fan-like tail.

Goldfish colors should be bright, dense, and even all over the body.

Handle your goldfish gently when you must. Keep handling to a minimum.

Under a microscope, you can see rings—one for each year of life—on the scales of a goldfish.

The body of the goldfish is covered with protective slime. Handling removes some of the slime and leaves the fish open to infection.

Spirulina algae will help bring out the best colors of your goldfish.

The goldfish's color intensifies in direct relationship to the amount of natural sunlight it is exposed to.

Goldfish are the traditional Chinese ornamental fish and all the goldfish today are of Chinese origin.

FINE FLOWING FINS

All fish have fins and goldfish are no exception. In fact, the fins are part and parcel of what makes the goldfish so attractive. There are many different tail and fin types, each developed through generations of careful selective breeding.

← Fantails can have normal or telescoped eyes. The color can be either nacreous or metallic and they are available in a full range of colors. The double tail is very long and flowing.

← The dorsal fin is a good indicator of the health of the fish. If it is held erect, the fish is in good form, but a folded fin can mean trouble.

Pearlscale orandas with the typical oranda headgrowth. ←

Pearlscales can have short butterfly tails like lionheads or longer tails like orandas.

A telescope pompon with fantail. ◀

◀ Blue-scale oranda. All the fins of the oranda are long and full.

← A moor goldfish with broadtail which is square-cut like a veiltail.

Fantails have an egg-shaped body with double anal and caudal fins.

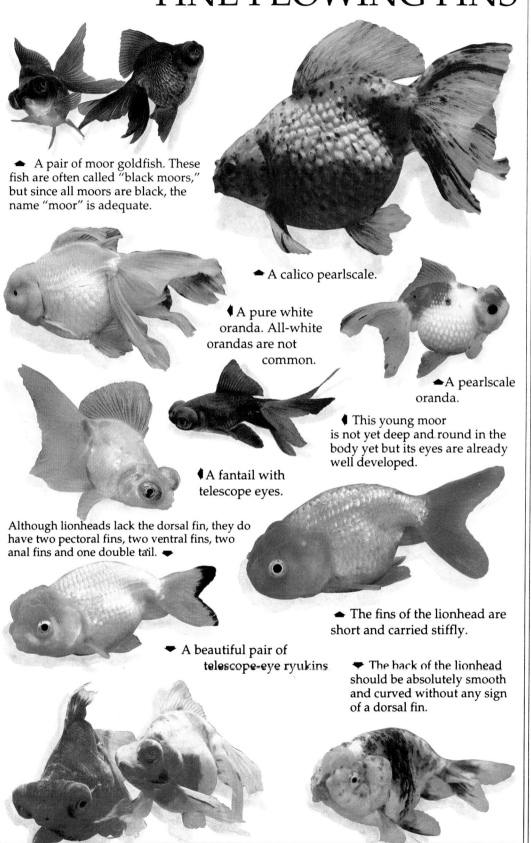

A pair of moor goldfish. These fish are often called "black moors," but since all moors are black, the name "moor" is adequate.

A calico pearlscale.

A pure white oranda. All-white orandas are not common.

A pearlscale oranda.

This young moor is not yet deep and round in the body yet but its eyes are already well developed.

A fantail with telescope eyes.

Although lionheads lack the dorsal fin, they do have two pectoral fins, two ventral fins, two anal fins and one double tail.

The fins of the lionhead are short and carried stiffly.

A beautiful pair of telescope-eye ryukins

The back of the lionhead should be absolutely smooth and curved without any sign of a dorsal fin.

FINE FLOWING FINS

There are over 100 different varieties of goldfish and a few more appear each year. Of these 100 varieties, 10 or 15 of the best sellers can be found in pet shops that cater to goldfish hobbyists. There is a goldfish for every fancy. Some people specialize and keep only one or two favorite types and work to better the strain, while others are fascinated by all the different varieties and like to try to develop new strains.

The comet has a more stream-lined shape than the common goldfish and the same type fins but longer. The comet is a fast swimmer and makes an ideal pond fish.

A red and white common goldfish that is suited for any environment, pond or aquarium.

There is a big contrast between the finnage of these fantails and the other fish on this page.

The most popular variety of the singletailed goldfish is the Bristol shubunkin. This fish has nice blues and reds from being kept outside in natural sunlight.

The common goldfish is the basic, down-to-earth, unaltered goldfish.

The common goldfish is a well-proportioned sturdily built fish. The fins are sturdy and rounded. The tail is short with moderate forking.

A goldfish's colors intensify with age, so a light gold-colored fish could deepen in color with time and proper feeding.

The common goldfish has a streamlined, torpedo-shaped body and relatively short fins. The colors run the gamut—red, orange, yellow, blue, brown, calico, white, and black.

FINE FLOWING FINS

The fin on the fish's back is called the dorsal fin. The fins on the sides are called the pectoral fins. The front two fins on the underside of the fish are called the ventral fins. The rear two fins are called the anal fins, and finally, the tail is called the caudal fin.

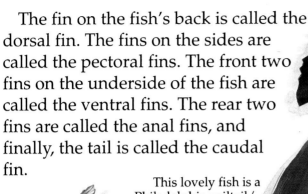

This lovely fish is a Philadelphia veiltail/ryukin cross. The Philadelphia veiltail has a very distinct drop to the caudal fin.

This red oranda, called the "Sunrise Oranda," sports excellent color and a well-developed tail.

The tosakin is fabulous for viewing from above. They are also called curly-tailed fantails for the shape of the tail.

A red Chinese lionhead with excellent headgrowth. The butterfly-tail of the lionhead attaches to a dropped caudal fin.

Tricolor (white, black, red) fantail.

This is a matte-scaled shubunkin. The fish almost appears scaleless, a rare feature for a shubunkin.

Fantail goldfish with metallic scales.

This is a major award-winning tricolor butterfly-tail telescope-eye with symmetrical eyes and a beautiful tail.

FINE FLOWING FINS

The different fins each serve a purpose. The pectoral and ventral fins control up and down movements of the fish and stabilize the fish at a certain depth. The air bladder works with the pectoral and anal fins. To sink in the water, the air bladder is contracted. When the air bladder is expanded it helps the fish to rise. The pectoral fins are used for upward motion and the ventral fins are in charge of downward motion. The dorsal and anal fins are used for balance.

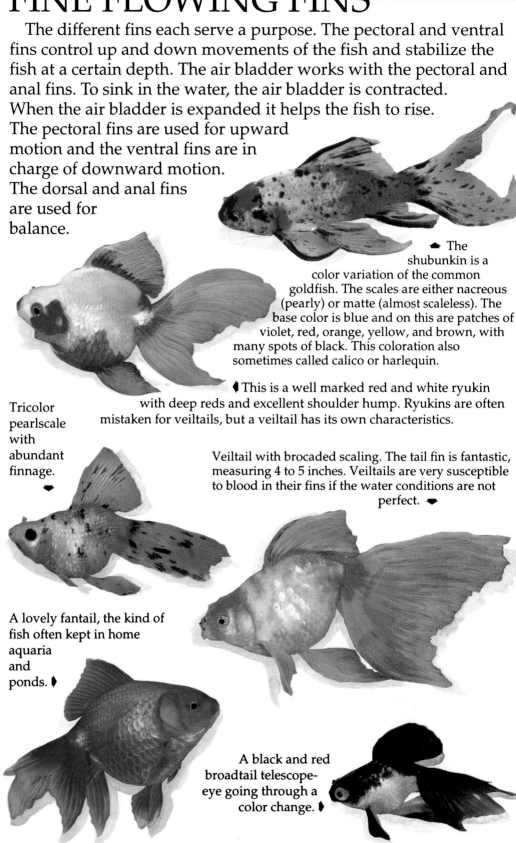

◄ The shubunkin is a color variation of the common goldfish. The scales are either nacreous (pearly) or matte (almost scaleless). The base color is blue and on this are patches of violet, red, orange, yellow, and brown, with many spots of black. This coloration also sometimes called calico or harlequin.

◀ This is a well marked red and white ryukin with deep reds and excellent shoulder hump. Ryukins are often mistaken for veiltails, but a veiltail has its own characteristics.

Tricolor pearlscale with abundant finnage. ➡

Veiltail with brocaded scaling. The tail fin is fantastic, measuring 4 to 5 inches. Veiltails are very susceptible to blood in their fins if the water conditions are not perfect. ➡

A lovely fantail, the kind of fish often kept in home aquaria and ponds. ▶

A black and red broadtail telescope-eye going through a color change. ▶

FINE FLOWING FINS

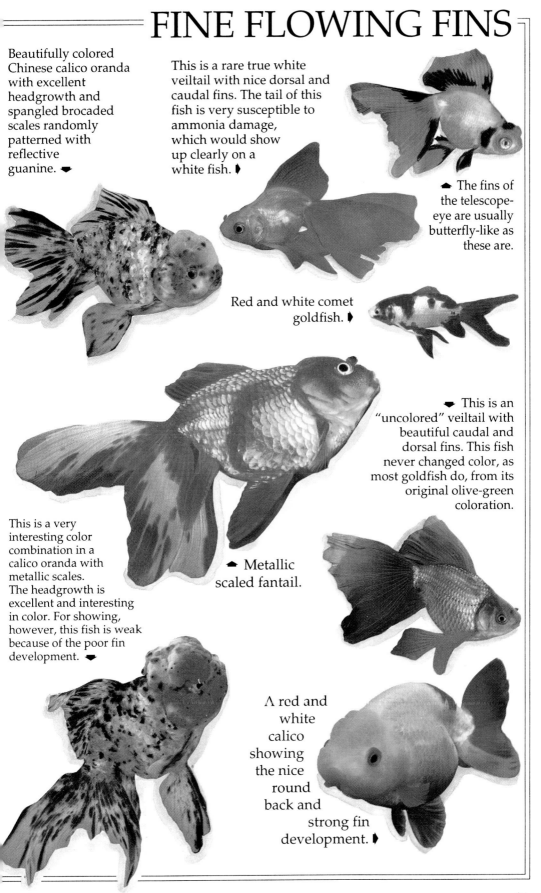

Beautifully colored Chinese calico oranda with excellent headgrowth and spangled brocaded scales randomly patterned with reflective guanine. ◄

This is a rare true white veiltail with nice dorsal and caudal fins. The tail of this fish is very susceptible to ammonia damage, which would show up clearly on a white fish. ▶

◄ The fins of the telescope-eye are usually butterfly-like as these are.

Red and white comet goldfish. ▶

◄ This is an "uncolored" veiltail with beautiful caudal and dorsal fins. This fish never changed color, as most goldfish do, from its original olive-green coloration.

This is a very interesting color combination in a calico oranda with metallic scales. The headgrowth is excellent and interesting in color. For showing, however, this fish is weak because of the poor fin development. ◄

◄ Metallic scaled fantail.

A red and white calico showing the nice round back and strong fin development. ▶

THE EYES HAVE IT

The goldfish is the only species of fish that has been bred for eye type. The normally eyed goldfish is like any other fish, but the orbs on some of these fish are...out of sight!

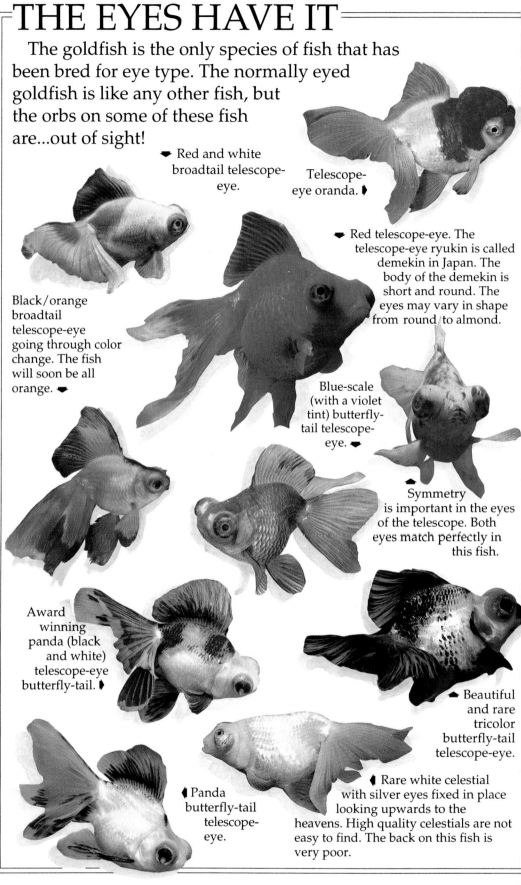

← Red and white broadtail telescope-eye.

Telescope-eye oranda. ▶

← Red telescope-eye. The telescope-eye ryukin is called demekin in Japan. The body of the demekin is short and round. The eyes may vary in shape from round to almond.

Black/orange broadtail telescope-eye going through color change. The fish will soon be all orange. ←

Blue-scale (with a violet tint) butterfly-tail telescope-eye. ←

▲ Symmetry is important in the eyes of the telescope. Both eyes match perfectly in this fish.

Award winning panda (black and white) telescope-eye butterfly-tail. ▶

← Beautiful and rare tricolor butterfly-tail telescope-eye.

◀ Panda butterfly-tail telescope-eye.

◀ Rare white celestial with silver eyes fixed in place looking upwards to the heavens. High quality celestials are not easy to find. The back on this fish is very poor.

THE EYES HAVE IT

The "eye-type" goldfish are not suited to outdoor ponds. Their eyes are too delicate and they require the special attention available only in the aquarium.

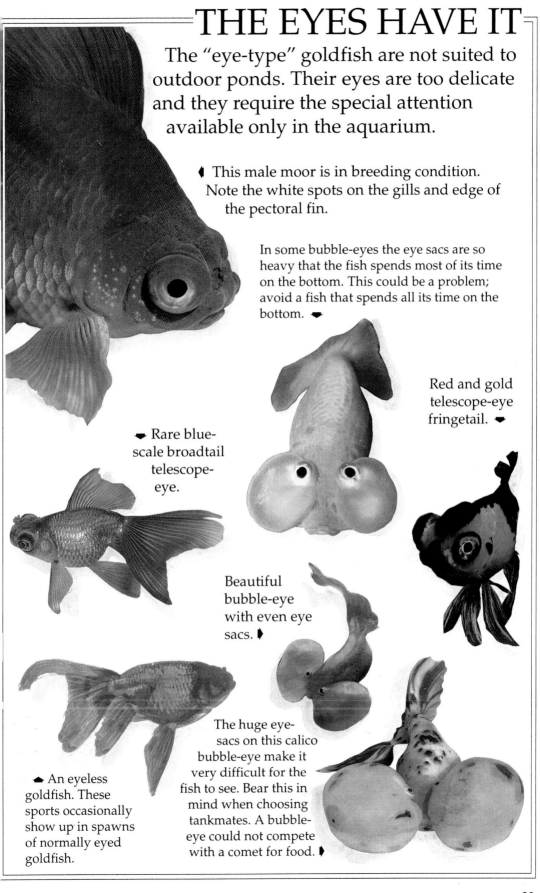

◀ This male moor is in breeding condition. Note the white spots on the gills and edge of the pectoral fin.

In some bubble-eyes the eye sacs are so heavy that the fish spends most of its time on the bottom. This could be a problem; avoid a fish that spends all its time on the bottom. ➡

Red and gold telescope-eye fringetail. ➡

➡ Rare blue-scale broadtail telescope-eye.

Beautiful bubble-eye with even eye sacs. ▶

➡ An eyeless goldfish. These sports occasionally show up in spawns of normally eyed goldfish.

The huge eye-sacs on this calico bubble-eye make it very difficult for the fish to see. Bear this in mind when choosing tankmates. A bubble-eye could not compete with a comet for food. ▶

THE EYES HAVE IT

The goldfish eye-types fascinate some people...and they make others nervous. It is hard to believe that there can be a fish like a bubble-eye. The water-filled sacs just beneath the eyes make these fish look like they're from outer space!

This is a telescope-eye oranda. The white on the cap is *not* fungus and shouldn't be treated with medications. It is a normal feature of the growth of the cap. ▶

◀ The bubble-eye's main feature is the fluid-filled sac under each eye. The sacs sway as the fish swims and in an adult, the sac can actually dwarf the fish. The bubble-eye, like the lionhead, does not have a dorsal fin as this would detract from its main feature, the eye sac.

The broadtail moor is a variety of the veiltail with telescope-eyes. Telescope-eyes bulge outward as spheres and should be equal on both sides. Moors are always black. This particular specimen has pompons as well. ◀

THE EYES HAVE IT

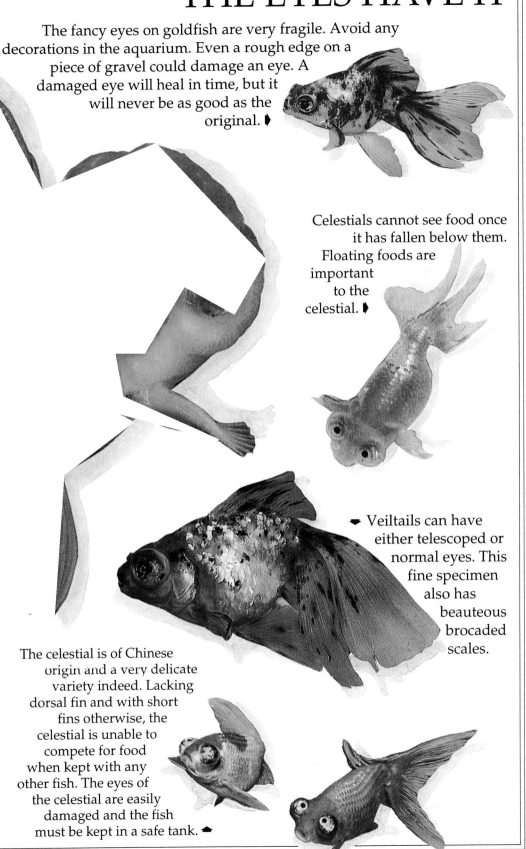

The fancy eyes on goldfish are very fragile. Avoid any decorations in the aquarium. Even a rough edge on a piece of gravel could damage an eye. A damaged eye will heal in time, but it will never be as good as the original. ▶

Celestials cannot see food once it has fallen below them. Floating foods are important to the celestial. ▶

◀ Veiltails can have either telescoped or normal eyes. This fine specimen also has beauteous brocaded scales.

The celestial is of Chinese origin and a very delicate variety indeed. Lacking dorsal fin and with short fins otherwise, the celestial is unable to compete for food when kept with any other fish. The eyes of the celestial are easily damaged and the fish must be kept in a safe tank. ▲

THE EYES HAVE IT

The eyes of the goldfish are similar to those of most other vertebrates. They are believed to be somewhat nearsighted. When goldfish are searching for food, the sense of smell seems to be more important than their sight.

Red and black butterfly-tail telescope-eye. Young fish like this eventually lose the black color and become solid orange. ➤

Fantastic red and white telescope-eyed oranda with the eyes protruding *out* from the head-growth. ▶

Gold telescope-eye butterfly-tail. ➤

Chocolate telescope-eye with pompons. ▶

An award winning black and gold telescope-eye butterfly-tail with nice, symmetrical eyes and a very nice butterfly tail. ➤

A black and red telescope-eye broadtail with an interesting color pattern. ▶

A perky pair of calico telescope-eye broadtails. ▶

This red and white butterfly-tail has symmetrical orange-encircled telescoped eyes.

THE EYES HAVE IT

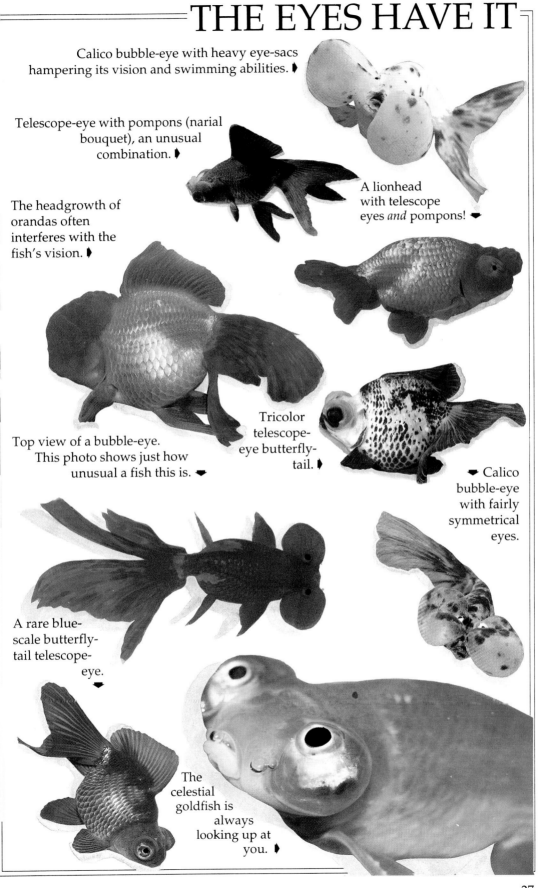

Calico bubble-eye with heavy eye-sacs hampering its vision and swimming abilities. ▶

Telescope-eye with pompons (narial bouquet), an unusual combination. ▶

The headgrowth of orandas often interferes with the fish's vision. ▶

A lionhead with telescope eyes *and* pompons! ➤

Top view of a bubble-eye. This photo shows just how unusual a fish this is. ➤

Tricolor telescope-eye butterfly-tail. ▶

➤ Calico bubble-eye with fairly symmetrical eyes.

A rare blue-scale butterfly-tail telescope-eye. ▼

The celestial goldfish is always looking up at you. ▶

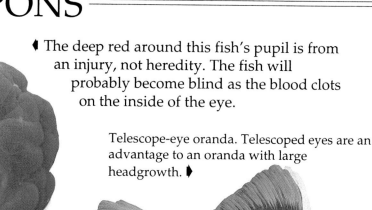

◀ The deep red around this fish's pupil is from an injury, not heredity. The fish will probably become blind as the blood clots on the inside of the eye.

Telescope-eye oranda. Telescoped eyes are an advantage to an oranda with large headgrowth. ▶

◀ Award winning red and white telescope broadtail. The beautiful markings and symmetry of the fins along with the red around the eye make this fish a real winner.

▲ A young telescope-eye pompon. Both the eyes and the narial bouquet will increase in size with age.

▲ Calico telescope-eye. The features of several goldfish types can be found on one fish as the result of careful breeding.

▲ This is a very attractive black and red telescope-eye with a ryukin-type body. The shoulder hump is being bred into the breed.

◀ A young chocolate blue-scaled telescope-eye pompon. This is an odd color combination.

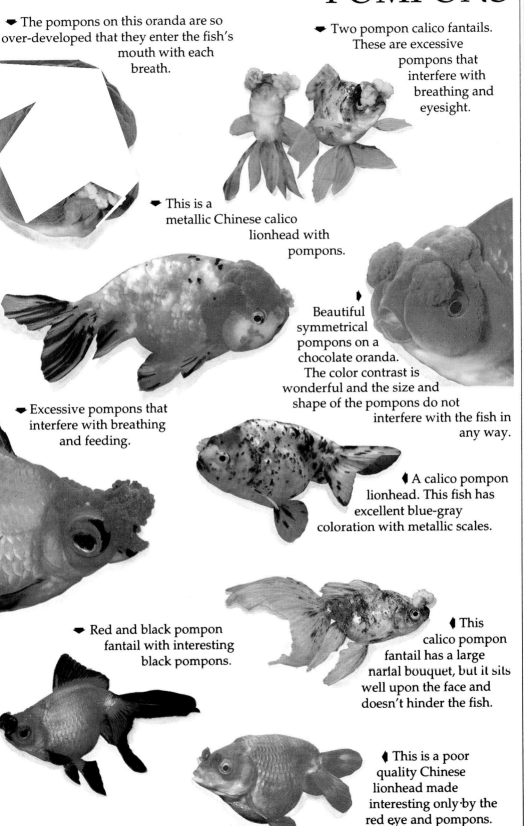

The pompons on this oranda are so over-developed that they enter the fish's mouth with each breath.

Two pompon calico fantails. These are excessive pompons that interfere with breathing and eyesight.

This is a metallic Chinese calico lionhead with pompons.

Beautiful symmetrical pompons on a chocolate oranda. The color contrast is wonderful and the size and shape of the pompons do not interfere with the fish in any way.

Excessive pompons that interfere with breathing and feeding.

A calico pompon lionhead. This fish has excellent blue-gray coloration with metallic scales.

Red and black pompon fantail with interesting black pompons.

This calico pompon fantail has a large narial bouquet, but it sits well upon the face and doesn't hinder the fish.

This is a poor quality Chinese lionhead made interesting only by the red eye and pompons.

ORANDAS

Orandas are the favorites of the goldfish hobby. Their rotund bodies, long fins, and big rounded heads make them very appealing. The headgrowth of the oranda usually covers the whole head. Adult orandas can weigh up to three pounds!

This huge oranda has great color. The deep red is most desirable and is the result of good genes, good food, and good light. ➤

A matte-scaled oranda. ➤

This black and red oranda has excellent conformation and balance, but will gradually lose the black color and become solid gold. ➤

➤ This is a very showy fish with its thick yellow headgrowth and good conformation.

The headgrowth is good on this calico oranda and the fins are nicely arranged, but the fish could use a little bit more blue in the color. ➤

This calico oranda could use more color, but the body and fins are great. ➤

◀ This oranda is called "Ancient Bronze" for the color of the body. Paired with the jet black fins and headgrowth, the bronze is exceptional.

ORANDAS

This is a doubletailed breed that has a short, round body with full flowing fins. The body should be muscular and as round as possible. Orandas are somewhat delicate in that very clean water is required to keep the headgrowth and fins in good condition. Because of their rounded bodies, they should also have a special diet.

The red-cap oranda. The cap should be confined to the head only and the body should be pure white. ▶

Blue-scale oranda going through a color change. The body is lightening and the headgrowth is turning yellow.

◀ A tricolor oranda with great patterning. The black streaks through the fins is very desirable.

◀ This is an unusual arrange-ment of color for a tricolor oranda, but very attractive.

◀ Tricolor oranda (red, black, and white) with beautiful headgrowth.

This is a champion Japanese calico oranda. ▼

Orandas and other round goldfish should have a diet high in greens to prevent blockage of their intestines.

ORANDAS

The oranda is essentially a veiltail with a lion head. This fish will likely turn all gold in time. The headgrowth is wonderful. ▶

Beautiful color and super headgrowth on a calico oranda. The blues and grays are excellent. The body is a little slim and could use some rounding out. ▶

◀ This is a very well-made calico oranda.

◀ Perfect form— body, fins, and headgrowth— on an orange oranda.

▶ "White cap" is not an official goldfish strain, but this fish certainly has one!

◀ Excellent calico oranda with very good coloring and nice metallic scales and finnage.

The headgrowth on this calico oranda is very small. This fish would be inexpensive to purchase. ◀

◀ A perfect oranda look!

This lovely tricolor oranda looks as if it wiggles through the water thanks to its short tail and golf-ball body. ▶

While the small bits of brown on the body are considered defects, this is a very nice young blue-scale oranda with nice head-growth and body shape. ▶

Nacreous white and gold oranda. ▶

Sarassa (red and white) oranda.
▼

◀ Headgrowth reflects not only age, but genetics and water quality as well.

▶
The red headgrowth against the white body provides stunning contrast in red and white orandas.

▶
This award winning oranda shows even headgrowth with nice balance to body and fins.

33

LIONHEADS

Lionheads and ranchus are dorsalless breeds of goldfish with large headgrowth. They are very similar in appearance, but the back of the ranchu displays a sharp downward angle just before it reaches the tail. The back outline of the lionhead is straighter, but it still curves into the tail. The ranchu has a double tail and the lionhead has a butterfly tail.

◆ A red lionhead with classic lionhead looks: no dorsal, small butterfly tail, and round little body.

◆ Marigold lionhead.

◀ Fantastic 5-year-old male "edonoshiki," or calico ranchu. This fish has a good color pattern and deep colors.

◆ Red and white metallic-scaled Chinese lionhead with a weak caudal peduncle and tail.

◀ Metallic lionhead with an uneven back.

The lionhead's hood should be as even as possible and should cover the entire head but not the eyes. The hood takes up to three years to mature. ◆

◆ The lionhead is a very exotic fish indeed. So called for the hood, or wen, that resembles the mane of the male lion, lionheads are called ranchus in Japan.

The body of the lionhead is an slightly elongated egg shape. ◆

LIONHEADS

The Japanese ranchu rarely has as large a headgrowth as the Chinese lionhead. This is, however, a fantastic 6-inch fish with excellent color and shape. ▶

▼Lionheads can be kept in a pond during the summer months, but must be brought indoors as winter approaches.

▼ Red and white metallic Chinese lionhead with a very nice color pattern.

▶ This is a very young edonoshiki with little headgrowth. Both the body and the headgrowth will develop as the fish matures.

At three months of age this ranchu is already starting to develop the characteristics of its race. ◀

▼Ranchus are not fast swimmers because of their body shape and lack of dorsal fin.

◀The Japanese lionhead, or ranchu, differs from the Western variety in that the back is more domed and the caudal peduncle is somewhat more tilted downward. This gives the fish a decidedly "tucked" look.

LIONHEADS

◀ The oranda head is very different from the lion head. The headgrowth on orandas is usually confined to the top, whereas the lionheads headgrowth covers the face as well.

▶ The groove on the back of the lionhead is a definite flaw in an otherwise very nice fish.

This young edonoshiki's back is not perfect, but the bumps may fill out as it grows and becomes bulkier. ◀

◀ At 8 inches in total length, this is a fantastic ranchu. The headgrowth is superb, the back smooth, and the color exceptional.

◀ This is a small red and white Chinese lionhead which has won many awards.

▼ This is an extremely rare black ranchu with jet-black coloring. There are plenty of black lionheads, but black ranchus are rare.

There's only one word for this fish in the goldfish fancier's vocabulary: boring. The fish lacks color, intensity, headgrowth, back contour, and tail conformation. ▶

This is a major award winning black lionhead. His headgrowth is massive, crater-like, and thick. His body is muscular, very strong, and compressed with a perfectly smooth back, which is a combination of Chinese lionhead and ranchu as there is a definite drop to the caudal peduncle. It is strong and holds the tail well.

This baby ranchu shows tremendous potential. The headgrowth has already started. The back is very nice and there is great "prop" to the caudal peduncle.

Red and white metallic lionhead with a nice smooth back. The metallic scales are rare and very desirable.

Black is a difficult color to maintain in lionheads. Usually the black disappears during the color change.

The headgrowth on this baby ranchu is starting to thicken. No one can know for sure until the fish is mature just how it will turn out.

White on white with a bit of red in the tail.

Red and white Chinese lionhead.

The back of this young edonoshiki will smooth out as the fish ages.

This red lion-head's head is thicker than its body!

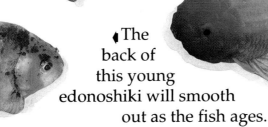

RYUKINS

The ryukin is a very round-bodied goldfish and in the highly developed humpbacked variety it looks like a ball with fins and head attached to it. The ryukin is one of the most popular goldfish breeds and is a very good breed for the beginner to start with. Ryukins are brightly colored and can be found in red, red and white, white, black, and the best calicos of any of the double tailed breeds.

☛Ryukins are some of the best calicos in the goldfish world. Calico ryukins are usually a bit weak in the shoulder, but this one is just fine.

A red and white ryukin with a good erect dorsal fin. This is an important feature.◗

◣Fantails and ryukins are basically the same variety as far as the tail goes, but it is the shoulder hump that distinguishes the ryukin.

This young ryukin has yet to develop the deep hump characteristic. ◗

◗ This is a true English veiltail. The body is egg-shaped like the ryukin, but notice the differences: the shoulder is smooth and the caudals are perfectly square from top to bottom. The pectorals and ventrals are very long and perfectly matched.

◣ This is a nice red and white ryukin, but fungus is stripping the slime coating off the tail. Treatment is necessary to help the fish return to health.

☛ A globe-eye or demekin.

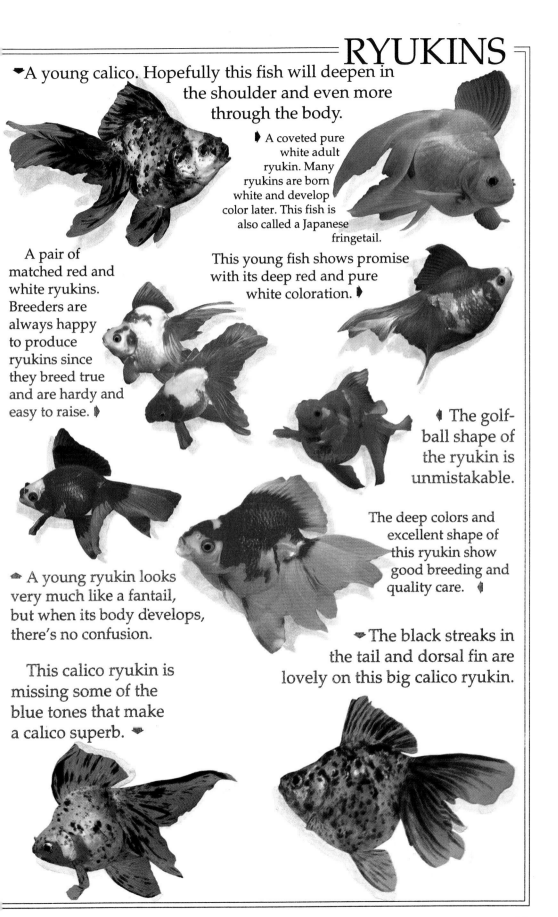

RYUKINS

→A young calico. Hopefully this fish will deepen in the shoulder and even more through the body.

▶ A coveted pure white adult ryukin. Many ryukins are born white and develop color later. This fish is also called a Japanese fringetail.

A pair of matched red and white ryukins. Breeders are always happy to produce ryukins since they breed true and are hardy and easy to raise. ▶

This young fish shows promise with its deep red and pure white coloration. ▶

◀ The golf-ball shape of the ryukin is unmistakable.

The deep colors and excellent shape of this ryukin show good breeding and quality care. ◀

→ A young ryukin looks very much like a fantail, but when its body develops, there's no confusion.

→The black streaks in the tail and dorsal fin are lovely on this big calico ryukin.

This calico ryukin is missing some of the blue tones that make a calico superb. →

39

GOLDFISH VARIETIES

Pearlscales are not among the hardier varieties of goldfish. They are unsuitable for the outdoor life and must be kept only with other slow-moving goldfish.

Pearlscales have scales that are raised like domes. The scales are very delicate and if a pearlscale loses one of its scales, the replacement is plain and not pearled. ▶

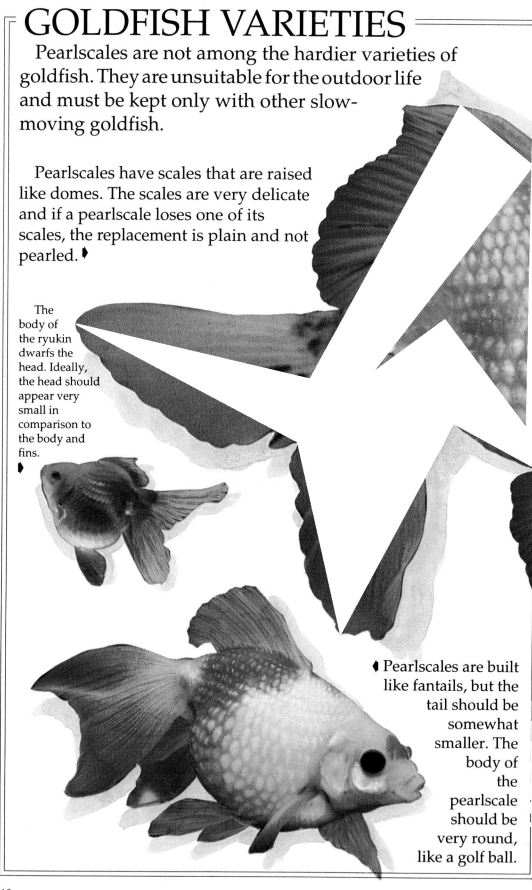

The body of the ryukin dwarfs the head. Ideally, the head should appear very small in comparison to the body and fins.
▶

◀ Pearlscales are built like fantails, but the tail should be somewhat smaller. The body of the pearlscale should be very round, like a golf ball.

GOLDFISH VARIETIES

Ryukins, like other goldfish, are descended from the crucian carp. The wild olive color is a reminder of this. ▶

◄ The pearly white on this fish is permanent. It's difficult to know until after the color change that occurs at about 6 months of age, just what color the fish will really be.

The rows of pearls on the body of the pearlscale curve to the shape of the fish.

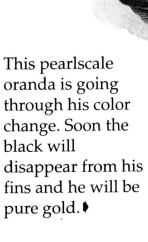

This pearlscale oranda is going through his color change. Soon the black will disappear from his fins and he will be pure gold. ▶

GOLDFISH VARIETIES

In Japan, the ryukin is called "onaga," which means long-tailed. The Japanese ryukins have deeper humps than the Chinese ryukins.

A red ryukin with a long tail. Many people mistake this for a veiltail, which it is not. A veiltail is a separate breed with its own characteristics and not just any fish with long fins.

A wonderful red and white ryukin with excellent conformation and deportment.

This is a red and white veiltail male ryukin. A ryukin can have a veil tail. The dorsal fin must be high and erect and the caudal square from lobe to lobe.

A black telescope eye, or demekin. It is essentially the same fish as a ryukin, but with globed eyes. This fish is a Japanese Grand Champion.

This is a very good quality fish, but it is still young and has not fully developed the desirable hump and long fins.

The hump on the ryukin deepens with age.

The fins on this fish are outstanding and the fish shows great promise.

Red like this is a product of good genes.

GOLDFISH VARIETIES

Demekins are best described as telescope-eyed ryukins.

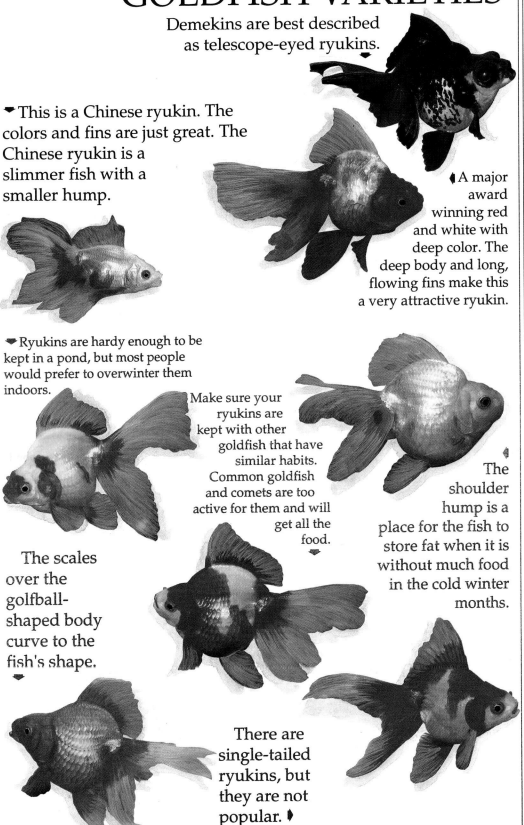

This is a Chinese ryukin. The colors and fins are just great. The Chinese ryukin is a slimmer fish with a smaller hump.

A major award winning red and white with deep color. The deep body and long, flowing fins make this a very attractive ryukin.

Ryukins are hardy enough to be kept in a pond, but most people would prefer to overwinter them indoors.

Make sure your ryukins are kept with other goldfish that have similar habits. Common goldfish and comets are too active for them and will get all the food.

The scales over the golfball-shaped body curve to the fish's shape.

The shoulder hump is a place for the fish to store fat when it is without much food in the cold winter months.

There are single-tailed ryukins, but they are not popular.

GOLDFISH CARE

Goldfish are among the easiest of all fishes to care for. They don't require elaborate aquarium setups. In fact, aquarium folklore is full of stories about goldfish kept in bowls for years with no water changes, only replacement of water lost to evaporation. Pity these poor creatures! No one knows how it felt to these fish, or if in their little fishy brains they wished every day for an end to their misery.

There are many different kinds of fish at your pet shop. These are oscars. They are often fed live common goldfish. ➥

➤ The container in which you keep your goldfish is very important. A pond or aquarium must have a large surface area to support the high oxygen requirements of goldfish.

▶ Bowls are *not* adequate homes for goldfish and any goldfish kept in a bowl will have a miserable life. Actually, goldfish can be kept in about any non-toxic container that is large enough.

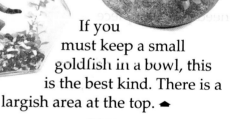

If you must keep a small goldfish in a bowl, this is the best kind. There is a largish area at the top. ➤

The modern planted aquarium is a beautiful decoration for your house. ▶

It is necessary to have a sturdy stand to place your aquarium upon. ➤

➤ The aquarium will be heavy when it is filled with water. Water weighs over 8 pounds a gallon. Decorations and gravel add extra weight.

GOLDFISH CARE

This is the TropiQuarium by Hagen. It is a sleek, good-looking aquarium design, perfect for goldfish. ➤

➤ Hagen has a full line of aquarium supplies to help you enjoy your fishkeeping hobby.

Acrylic tanks come in a variety of shapes. The model shown has rounded corners. The hood is specially designed to fit this size and style of tank. ➤

Starter kits contain everything you need to start up your first aquarium. You can also buy the equipment you need piece by piece. ➤

➤ A good pet shop will have all the equipment you need and the employees will help you choose the pieces that are needed for your situation.

◀ Once you have an aquarium, stand, hood and light, filter, and gravel, you are ready to get started!

◀ This unique aquarium is divided so you actually have three aquaria in one. You can put different kinds of fish in each section.

▶ Cycle by Hagen helps establish beneficial bacteria in your filter.

GOLDFISH CARE

▶ Every tank should have a hood to prevent excess water evaporation...and to prevent dust and fumes from getting into the water.

A hood should fit properly on the aquarium so there is no chance of it falling into the water.

◆ Gravel should be rounded to prevent damage to the delicate mouths of your fish.

◆ A bed of gravel will help keep your aquarium clean.

There are many decorative ornaments for use in your aquarium. Just be sure they don't have any sharp edges.

◆ A glass tank cover is necessary if you decide you don't want to use a full hood.

▶ Any of the ornaments you will find in your pet shop are safe to use in the aquarium. It's tempting to use rocks or driftwood you find outdoors, but they could be toxic to your fish.

◆ If you overcrowd the tank, there will be little room left for your fishes!

◆ Arrange your plants and decorations before you put the water in the tank. It's a lot easier to move things around without the water.

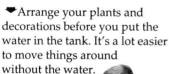

◆ Plastic plants are attractive and functional in the aquarium. The goldfish will pick at the algae that forms on the leaves.

GOLDFISH CARE

An "algae magnet" is used to clean the glass of algae. Clean glass makes your aquarium more enjoyable. If you use window cleaner to clean the outside of the glass, you must be careful that none of it gets into the water. It's best to spray the cloth and then clean the glass.

A gravel washer will make changing your water and cleaning your gravel a snap. ▶

Algae scrapers are for cleaning the inside glass of the aquarium. Use this tool often.

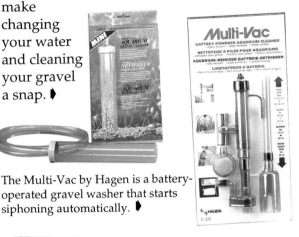

The Multi-Vac by Hagen is a battery-operated gravel washer that starts siphoning automatically. ▶

Fin Care by Hagen is a soothing liquid that you should use every time you have to move your fish. At the first sign of fin irritation, add a dose to the water and help your fish heal.

The Hagen Algae Scraper has a planting tong on the other end for replacing plants and ornaments that have strayed from their proper places in the tank.

This is handy siphon starter will get the siphon going on your hose every time you want to change your water.

The best thing you can do for your fish is learn how to properly care for them. Read aquarium books and magazines like *Tropical Fish Hobbyist*. Even if every article isn't about the kind of fish you are keeping, there will be tips and suggestions you can apply to your own situation. ▶

GOLDFISH CARE

To easily catch a fish, remove the tank hood and view the fish from the side, not from the top as shown here. Some people "train" their fish not to be afraid of the net by putting a little food in the net and leaving it in the aquarium for a little while. ➤

Sooner or later you are going to want to catch your fish. To do this you are going to have to have a net. You won't be able to catch a fish by chasing it around with your hands. Make sure the net you buy is large enough to easily catch your largest fish without damaging it.

The net should be made of soft nylon with large enough holes to allow the water to pass through easily. The small fine-meshed nets you will see in the store are for catching and rinsing brine shrimp and the nets are very slow in the water.

The handle of the net should be long enough for your to capture a fish in any part of the tank. ➤

➤ Nets are available with different size mesh pockets and different length handles. Get a small net for a small tank and a large one for a large tank. The bigger the net, the easier it is to catch the fish!

EASY CATCH NET
by HAGEN

➤ Sometimes it is useful to have a goldfish bowl to hold a new fish in quarantine to make sure it is healthy before you put it into your established aquarium.

◀ When moving your fish into your aquarium, give it a chance to adjust slowly to new water conditions such as temperature, pH, and even cleanliness.

You can use a goldfish bowl to "acclimate" the fish to your water. Put the goldfish and the transport water into the bowl and slowly add water from your aquarium to fill the bowl. Then you can net the fish and put it into the aquarium. Throw away the water. ▲

PUMPS & FILTERS

Each aquarium can adequately maintain about one inch of fish for each gallon of water—that means ten small fishes in a ten-gallon tank. This usually does not present a satisfactory arrangement as most people want more life in their aquarium. To increase the aquarium's capacity to sustain fish life it is necessary to aerate the water, thereby adding oxygen and removing carbon dioxide. This is done with a pump. A filter, always activated by a pump, removes harmful chemicals, debris and even toxic gases. Therefore, a pump and filter are necessities that should be bought when you buy your original tank set up.

Hagen has an air pump that is battery powered. This is useful for emergencies or when taking your fish on a long trip. ➤

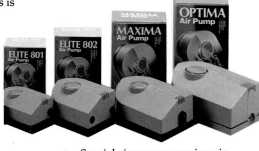

➤ Special air pumps running via vibrating membranes are available in at least 4 different sizes. Photo by Hagen.

➤ Air pumps running small inside filters must be matched. You don't want excessive air to interfere with the operation of the filter.

▶ It's not how large the aquarium is that is important, but how DEEP it is, as depth creates back pressure and a more powerful pump is needed for deep tanks.

➤ Never remove a submergible electrical pump (or heater) unless it is disconnected.

Hagen has a series of more powerful and adjustable pumps. ➤

A new kind of filtration based upon bacterial activity plus mechanical filtration is called *WET-DRY* filtration. The Bio- Life Hagen is a good one which I have used successfully on a 20-gallon tank for over a year without changing water. ▶

◀ Teach your children to keep their hands out of the tank especially when electrical gadgets are alive.

PUMPS & FILTERS

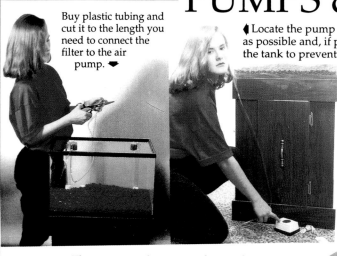

Buy plastic tubing and cut it to the length you need to connect the filter to the air pump. ➡

◀ Locate the pump as close to the tank as possible and, if possible, above the tank to prevent siphoning of the water should the pump fail.

▶ There are many qualities in plastic tubing. The Hagen Silicone is the highest quality. Buy it in long lengths as it must be changed periodically.

➡ There are attachments and cartridges available for all power heads and under gravel filters. It can double the filtering capacity of your pump/filter.

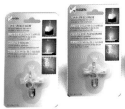

Airline tubing comes in various lengths and qualities. You need about 20 feet to set up the usual aquarium. ◀

Gang valves help you adjust the air pump to various outlets in filters and ornaments. ▶

Activated carbon removes harmful gases like carbon dioxide, as well as medications that discolor the water. ▶

➡ There are many filters that accommodate the addition of filter charcoal or activated carbon. You should use activated carbon and change it weekly.

Poly wool is a filter material which physically removes suspended particles passing through the filter. It is necessary to change or wash the wool every week or so depending on the amount of debris accumulated. ▶

The Aqua-Clear Power Filter by Hagen can be charged with activated carbon and *poly* filter wool. ▶

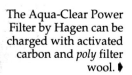

UNDER GRAVEL FILTERS

Undergravel filters fit under the gravel and should cover the complete bottom. This is the lazy-man's filter since there is no carbon or wool to change, but it has limited effectiveness.

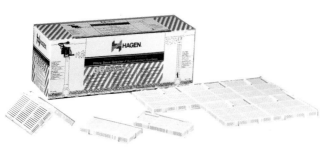

Hagen has a do-it-yourself undergravel filter kit. The squares interlock and each square is sturdy and self supported making it possible to use it again for a different size aquarium.

Undergravel filters should fit the bottom of the tank perfectly. The tank must be empty when it is fitted.

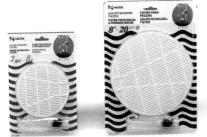

◀ Hagen even makes undergravel filters for goldfish bowl or other round-bottomed aquariums.

The aerating columns of the undergravel filters should not rise above the top of the tank. ▶

➭Undergravel filters should be equipped with aerating columns like the ClearFlow by Hagen.

➭Once the undergravel filter is in place with the aerating columns set, the gravel can be added. The gravel should be about two inches deep to provide proper filtration.

➭ Powerheads attached to the aerating column can increase the movement through the filter by 10 times or more.

➭Don't ruin everything by adding water to a set up aquarium in a vigorous manner which uproots the plants and disturbs the gravel.

WHY GOLDFISH?

Goldfish are most often the first aquarium fish that a young person is exposed to...be it a gift, a prize, or the result of putting together his pennies to buy his own special pet. The desire to keep aquaria is strong in many people, people who are perhaps instinctively responding to a personal need for a tool for meditation and relaxation. Goldfish keeping fulfills this need splendidly. Research has shown that people who spend 10 minutes gazing into a peaceful aquarium feel less pain and anxiety during dental procedures. Hospital rooms equipped with aquaria are found to be places where visitors stay longer and patients heal faster. Watching an aquarium will also reduce elevated blood pressure.

Keeping an aquarium is a family affair. Gary shows his and a neighbor's kids how to transfer a fish from an isolation bowl to the main aquarium.

Even without the health benefits, aquarium-gazing is a delightful way to spend spare time. Newborns, not yet able to focus their eyes, are alert to the sounds of an aquarium. As the days pass and vision becomes more focussed, you will see the baby's eyes following the movements of the fish in the tank. Big excitement for both baby and parents! The graceful movements of the fish can be mesmerizing, leaving the person relaxed and refreshed after just a few minutes in front of the aquarium. Not simply a spectator sport, the aquarium and its attendant responsibilities teach us important lessons about the nature of water and the needs of living things.

WHY GOLDFISH?

There are many little tricks that you will learn as you keep goldfish. For instance, you may find that it is easier to change your water if you hang the hose out a nearby window and drain the water into the garden. Everyone develops their own style of fishkeeping and whatever works for you, and your fish, is all right.

◀Headgrowth of this quality can only be achieved with super care and attention to diet and attention to water quality.

◆ Goldfish are very fond of plants. They like to eat them. Vallisneria is one plant that is too tough for them though, so if you want a nice plant that will last in the goldfish tank, try Vallisneria.

◆ If a goldfish that has been kept indoors or in a shady location is moved into the sunlight, the fins and even sometimes the entire fish can become sunburned and blackened.

◆ The term "singletail" is meant to describe the fish has the more usual single tail as opposed to the fancier tailed varieties.

Pompons have a growth of the nasal region called a "narial bouquet." The extent of the growth is highly variable. On some fish they are insignificant and on others they dangle in front of the mouth and are sucked in and out with each breath. ▶

The globe-eye has unusual eyes that protrude from the head in a cone shape. The body and fins are similar to the veiltail, but the caudal fin is forked. ▶

FEEDING GOLDFISH

The amount and kind of foods you offer your goldfish are very important to their health and growth. Goldfish are the easiest of fish to feed as they will eat almost anything almost any time.

The frozen foods department at your pet shop makes it possible for you to give your fish a variety of frozen foods year round. San Francisco Bay Brand puts out all kinds of great foods like bloodworms, brine shrimp, mosquito larvae, and more. ◆

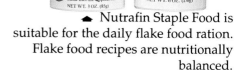

Nutrafin Staple Food is suitable for the daily flake food ration. Flake food recipes are nutritionally balanced.

Goldfish flake food is available in all sizes. The giant economy size is handy if you keep a large number of fish, but for freshness' sake only buy as much as you will use in a month or two. ◆

◆ Brine shrimp hatchers like this one from San Francisco Bay Brand make it easy to offer newly hatched brine shrimp to your goldfish fry. You can even grow the brine shrimp out for your older fish.

◆ Red grubs are an interesting appetizer for your goldfish. The key to feeding goldfish, or any fishes for that matter, is variety.

FEEDING GOLDFISH

To maintain good health in goldfish, offer them a diet high in carbohydrates, especially vegetable foods with additional protein foods during conditioning for breeding. What this means is that you should give them a moderate amount of live foods in the spring. Goldfish have very small stomachs. Their digestive processes are almost completely intestinal. Because of this unusual arrangement, goldfish eat almost constantly. Even so, don't overfeed. It's better to have some soft-leaved plants growing in the aquarium for snacking purposes.

◄ Hand feeding is a bonus of goldfish keeping. It's a big thrill when your fish takes food from your fingers.

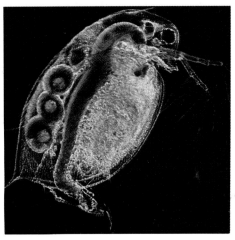

Fresh, clean tubifex worms are accepted by most goldfish and are easily purchased. Avoid high-protein foods during the winter if your fish are outdoors. Use a lighter alternative instead like flake food to keep your pond water sweet. ◄

◄ Daphnia and other small crustaceans are favorite foods of goldfish. Don't feed outdoor fish during very cold weather. Food will remain uneaten and decompose. This will reduce the amount of oxygen in the pond and cause tremendous water quality problems.

Goldfish will constantly pick at the gravel—ever on the lookout for missing morsels. Avoid overfeeding, however, as uneaten foods will cause problems with water quality. ◄

GOLDFISH

The care you give your goldfish will be rewarded many times over. Goldfish keeping is fun and educational for the whole family.

▲ This trio of young ryukins are from the same spawn. When the young all look alike, you know the strain is well set and their offspring will all look alike as well.

▲ This beautiful oranda will lose its black coloration and soon be all red.

▶ This pair of white orandas show small amounts of red, but this doesn't detract from the beauty of the fish.

GOLDFISH

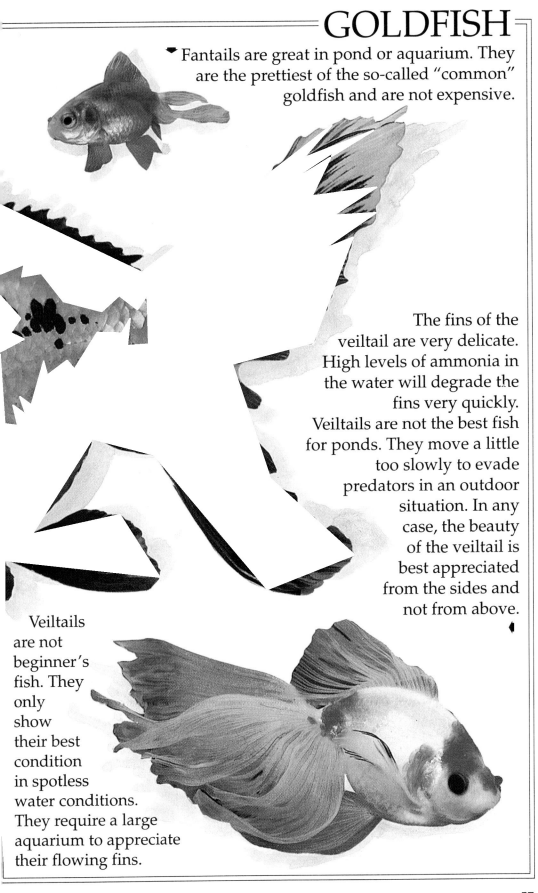

Fantails are great in pond or aquarium. They are the prettiest of the so-called "common" goldfish and are not expensive.

The fins of the veiltail are very delicate. High levels of ammonia in the water will degrade the fins very quickly. Veiltails are not the best fish for ponds. They move a little too slowly to evade predators in an outdoor situation. In any case, the beauty of the veiltail is best appreciated from the sides and not from above.

Veiltails are not beginner's fish. They only show their best condition in spotless water conditions. They require a large aquarium to appreciate their flowing fins.

BREEDING GOLDFISH

Breeding goldfish is fun and easy. The importance of conditioning your fish cannot be underestimated. Conditioning should be an ongoing effort. To condition goldfish for breeding, give them perfect water, good food, seasonal temperature changes, and plenty of space.

The development of this fish took many generations of careful selection. Maintain the integrity of the strains and try to improve them where you can.

Fast-swimming goldfish may need more space for spawning than slower fancier types.

A pearlscale oranda. The male is distinguished by white bumps on his face and the first rays of the pectoral fins.

There is an 88% probability of obtaining at least one pair in a group of six fish.

While this fish may be pretty at first glance (and I certainly thought so), experts would call his dorsal and tail fins weak and unworthy to reproduce.

Good quality food of the proper kind and in the proper amounts is a must for conditioning goldfish. Just before and during the spawning season a food high in protein, preferable live, should be fed to your spawners at least once a day.

BREEDING GOLDFISH

◀ The female goldfish will fill with eggs very quickly if the water temperature is about 60°F and begin spawning when it reaches about 68°F.

◀ The male chases the female and fertilizes the eggs as she throws them.

◀ Goldfish will spawn readily in a tank of about 30 gallons.

◀ As soon as they have finished spawning for the day, the goldfish will turn around and eat their own eggs.

Goldfish fry a few hours old. ▶

A plain comet goldfish will produce between 2000 and 5000 eggs per spawn. ◀

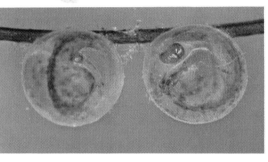

◀ The eyes of the fry are clearly visible in these eggs that will soon hatch.

Large fancy goldfish are more sedate in their courtship and spawning than the plain fish and produce fewer fry. ▶

All varieties of goldfish can interbreed. It is best, however, to leave the experiments to the experts and breed known varieties. ◀

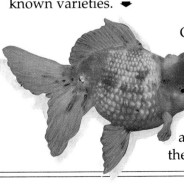

Goldfish can safely spend the winter in an outdoor pond as long as the water doesn't freeze solid to the bottom. Spawning will be an automatic springtime event as the water warms up. ▶

GOLDFISH

Ryukin.

Black Moor Goldfish.

Lionhead, or Ranchu. The size and shape of the head-growth depends on genetics, nutrition, and water quality.

Ryukins. Many Ryukins become more colorful as they age.

Pearl-scale Oranda. If a pearled scale is lost, the new scale will be normal, not pearl.

Veiltail Goldfish.

Jikin. The Jikin is usually bicolored.

Redcap Oranda.

Oranda. The Oranda always has a dorsal fin.

Pearlscale Oranda.

Black Oranda.

Oranda.

Chocolate Oranda.

The Chinese Lionhead.

Calico Telescope-eye.

Bubble-eye Goldfish. This fish could have been crossed with a Celestial in an effort to combine features of both.

Oranda. The headgrowth on Orandas increases with maturity.

Veiltail Oranda. Long-finned Goldfish need very clean water to prevent damage to the fins.

Oranda. Do not keep Orandas with fast-swimming fish as they are too slow to compete for food.

White Redcap Oranda. The contrast of white and red makes this a magnificent fish.

Redcap Oranda. The Redcap is one of the most popular of the Orandas.

Calico Oranda. The red in Calicos will intensify with a diet high in vegetable matter.

Bubble-eye Goldfish. The eye-sacs are filled with water.

Bubble-eye Goldfish. If the bubble is damaged it will grow back, but not as magnificently as the original.

GOLDFISH

Goldfish are hardy, long-lived pets. They are not tropical fish but are what are called temperate fish. This simply means that they are found in cool water. You won't need a heater in the aquarium when you keep Goldfish.

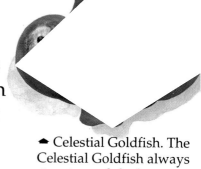

➤ Celestial Goldfish. The Celestial Goldfish always stare toward the heavens, hence the name "Celestial."

Common Goldfish. Common Goldfish are inexpensive, attractive, and very hardy—perfect starter fish for newcomers to the hobby. ➤

➤ Calico Ryukin. Calico describes the wonderful palette of colors on these fish, no two of which are exactly alike.

➤ Pearlscale. Each scale is raised and reflects light like the pearls for which this fish is named.

➤ Calico Oranda. The Japanese call this fish an Azumanishiki.

Ranchus. A Ranchu has a round, squat body and no dorsal fin.

◀ ➤ Celestials. Celestials have no dorsal fins and are sometimes called Deme-Ranchu.

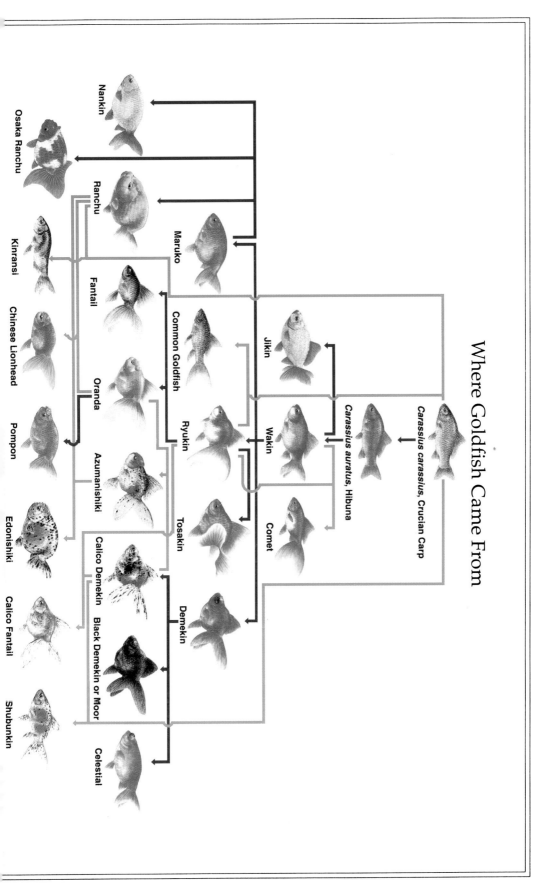

Where Goldfish Came From

Carassius carassius, Crucian Carp

Carassius auratus, Hibuna

Jikin

Wakin

Comet

Common Goldfish

Ryukin

Tosakin

Demekin

Maruko

Fantail

Oranda

Azumanishiki

Calico Demekin

Black Demekin or Moor

Nankin

Osaka Ranchu

Ranchu

Kinransi

Chinese Lionhead

Pompon

Edonishiki

Calico Fantail

Shubunkin

Celestial

INDEX